EDGE BOOKS

X-SPORTS

BMX RACING

BY ANN WEIL

CONSULTANT:
KEITH MULLIGAN
EDITOR / PHOTOGRAPHER
TRANSWORLD BMX MAGAZINE

Capstone
press

Mankato, Minnesota

Edge Books are published by Capstone Press
151 Good Counsel Drive, P.O. Box 669, Mankato, Minnesota 56002
www.capstonepress.com

Library of Congress Cataloging-in-Publication Data
Weil, Ann.
    BMX racing / by Ann Weil.
    p. cm.—(Edge books, X-sports)
    Includes bibliographical references and index.
    ISBN 0-7368-2709-9
    1. Bicycle motocross—Juvenile literature. [1. Bicycle motocross. 2. Bicycle racing.
    3. Extreme sports.] I. Title. II. Series.
  GV1049.3.W45 2005
  796.62—dc22   2003026310

Summary: Discusses the sport of BMX racing, including gear needed, moves, and
famous racers.

Editorial Credits
James Anderson, editor; Jason Knudson, designer; Jo Miller, photo researcher;
   Eric Kudalis, product planning editor

Photo Credits
All photos by TransWorld BMX/Keith Mulligan except page 6, by Bruce Mulligan.

The publisher does not endorse products whose logos may appear on objects in images in this book.

1 2 3 4 5 6 09 08 07 06 05 04

TABLE OF CONTENTS

CHAPTER 1

BMX RACING

Eight BMX racers line up behind the starting gate. A green light flashes, and the gate snaps down. The racers push on their pedals as hard as they can. Each rider wants to be the first out of the gate. Starting in front is easier than passing during the race.

Racers take off over jumps. Their bikes tilt sideways as they speed through steep berms. One rider spins out at the top of a berm. He falls and knocks over another racer. Both riders quickly get back on their bikes.

In less than one minute, the winner crosses the finish line. One race is over, but the next race is about to begin.

LEARN ABOUT:

- Early BMX riders
- Sponsors
- Downhill racing

BMX racers stay low during a race.

BICYCLE MOTOCROSS

BMX is short for bicycle motocross. Motocross riders race motorcycles on dirt tracks that have bumps, jumps, and turns. BMX is like motocross, only racers ride bicycles.

BMX began in the 1970s. Some kids in California raced their bikes on motocross tracks. The kids built their own track and invited their friends to join them.

The new sport caught on. More people raced BMX. People in many towns built BMX tracks. Bike companies made bikes and equipment just for BMX. Soon, BMX events were held around the world.

Most people who race BMX are amateurs. They enjoy the sport as a hobby. Some BMX racers are pros. They race for fun and money. These racers go from one big race to another. Some pro riders travel around the world.

Pro racers have sponsors. These companies pay racers for advertising their products. Sponsors also give riders bikes, clothing and equipment. Riders try to do well at big races to gain the attention of sponsors.

Amateur and pro riders take part in BMX races.

DOWNHILL BMX

In May 2000, the first pro downhill BMX race was held at Camp Woodward, Pennsylvania. Downhill BMX is now part of the X Games. Many people watch the X Games to see downhill BMX races.

Downhill BMX races take place on a fast track with tall berms and huge jumps. Riders can fly 40 feet (12 meters) off the jumps. Most downhill BMX tracks are about 1,500 feet (460 meters) long. Downhill BMX tracks are steep. Riders don't have to pedal much to keep going. The riders' momentum keeps them moving.

Downhill BMX is more dangerous than regular BMX racing. Some racers have broken bones during downhill BMX races. Robbie Miranda was knocked out during a downhill race at the 2001 X Games. He didn't wake up until other riders had finished the race. Luckily, Miranda was okay. He won the same event the following year.

Downhill BMX jumps are much higher than jumps on other BMX tracks.

EDGE FACT

Some downhill BMX races are called BMX Supercross.

CHAPTER 2

BMX GEAR

BMX racers need the right equipment to take part in races. BMX officials will not let riders race without safety equipment and pads.

BMX BIKES

BMX bikes are built to be strong and fast. They are made of a strong mixture of metals called chromoly.

BMX bikes have many important features. They have 20- or 24-inch (51- or 61-centimeter) wheels. Riders slow and stop their bikes with a hand brake. The brake lever is on the right side of the handlebar.

LEARN ABOUT:
- **Equipment**
- **Tires**
- **Pads**

BMX riders use proper equipment and safety gear.

Riders call their racing tires knobbies. These wide thick tires have bumps and grooves. They grip the dirt well so the bike doesn't lose traction during a race.

Some riders place pads on the handlebars, stem, and frame. These pads protect racers when they bump against the bike during a race.

SAFETY GEAR

Most racers crash or fall off their bikes often. They can get hurt if they are not prepared. Head injuries can be serious.

All racers must wear helmets. BMX riders wear full-face helmets. These helmets cover the ears and protect the entire face.

BMX racers wear lots of pads. Some racers wear knee and shin pads under their pants. Knee pads have a plastic cup that covers the knee. Shin pads protect the lower leg. Many riders also wear pads to protect their elbows and wrists.

EDGE FACT

A BMX race is called a moto. The winners of each moto get points that qualify them for the final races, called mains.

Racing pants and jerseys are called leathers. This protective clothing has built-in safety padding. Although they are called leathers, these clothes are made of nylon.

Some racers wear gloves that help them grip the handlebars. Gloves also protect their hands in case of a crash.

Racers also wear BMX shoes. These shoes grip the pedals. The tongue of the shoe is padded to protect the foot. Some shoes have a metal piece on the bottom that clicks into the pedal.

Riders wear full-face helmets.

BMX TRACK DIAGRAM

 Starting gate

 Roller

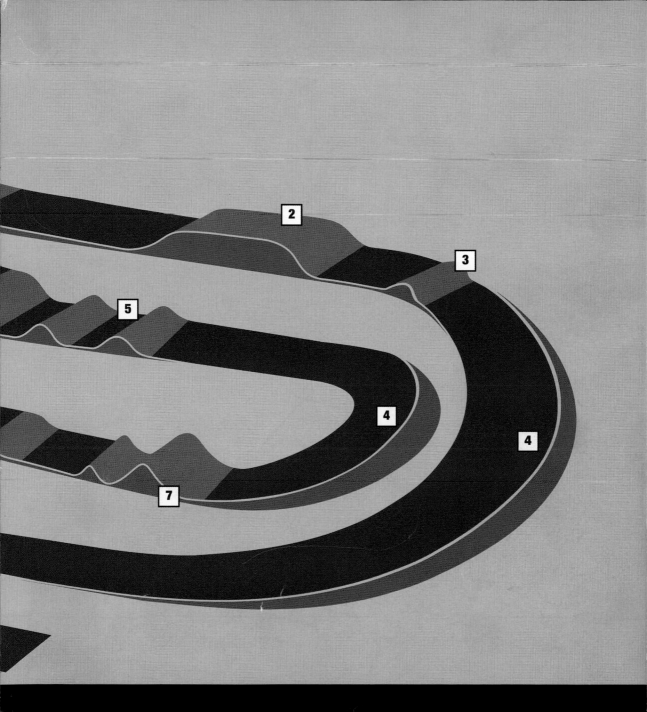

CHAPTER 3

BMX RACING MOVES

BMX tracks are 900 to 1,500 feet (275 to 460 meters) long. The tracks are made mostly of hard-packed dirt. Some tracks have asphalt hills and berms.

BMX tracks have jumps and other obstacles that test racers' skills. Downhill BMX tracks have higher berms and longer jumps.

GATE MOVES

Before racers get to the berms and jumps on a track, they need a good start to the race. Riders want to be the first out of the gate. Often, the first rider has a chance to hold the lead for the rest of the race.

LEARN ABOUT:

- Balancing on the gate
- Berms
- Doubles and tabletops

16

Racers balance on the gate to get a fast start.

Racers try to pass on berms.

Some racers stand up on their pedals just before the gate falls. This move is called balancing on the gate. Riders use this move to get going faster.

Snapping out of the gate is another way riders get a good start. Racers who snap out of the gate lean forward and push on the pedals at the same time.

RIDING THE BERM

After the gate is down, riders go over jumps. After the jumps, the first obstacle is often a turn. Most BMX turns are called berms. Berms are turns that are built up at a steep angle. Racers ride the berms at high speeds.

Berms have imaginary lines. Racers call these lines the outside, middle, and inside lines. Riders pay attention to the lines when they pass each other on the berms. Many racers like to start at the bottom of the inside. They then swoop up to the outside, or top line.

Riders enter or exit a berm in any line. Riders often enter and exit berms on different lines to keep other riders from passing.

JUMPS

     Racers launch off jumps on a BMX track. Some tracks are more difficult than others because they have higher jumps.

     Tracks have several types of jumps. Doubles are common jumps. A double is made of two jumps that are close together. Riders get air on the first jump. They try not to land until they have cleared the second jump.

Staying low over jumps helps riders keep up speed.

Doubles are not always the same size. A step-up is a double in which the second jump is higher than the first. Riders must have good speed when they approach a step-up. A step-down is the opposite of a step-up. The first jump in a step-down is higher.

Tabletops are jumps that are flat on top. Tabletops have steep front and back sides. Racers try to gain speed as they pedal up to the jump. Some riders try to fly across the tabletop and land on the other side of the jump. Others stay low and pedal across the top.

CHAPTER 4

FAMOUS PROS

A few of the best BMX racers make a career of riding bikes. They win prize money. Sponsors also pay them. A few pro BMX riders make as much as $300,000 a year.

No one starts out as a pro BMX rider. Riders need time, practice, and skill to make it to the top. Some pro riders do not ride well in their first races. Many pros say that practicing on their first bikes helped them become great riders.

LEARN ABOUT:
- **Record breakers**
- **World champions**
- **Comebacks**

Many amateur racers want to be pro riders.

SAMANTHA COOLS

Samantha Cools was the world's top-ranked junior woman BMX racer in 2002 and 2003. Cools is from Canada. She started racing BMX when she was just 4 years old. Her older brother was also a BMX rider. Cools says that when she was old enough to walk, she wanted to ride a bike.

When Cools was 10 years old, she raced in England at a world championship race. During the main race, she was in fourth place while she pedaled up to a double. She was the only one to clear the jump. She passed the first three racers and won her first world championship.

EDGE FACT

BMX racing will be a new event at the 2008 Olympic Games in Beijing, China.

Samantha Cools is a top-ranked female racer.

KYLE BENNETT

Kyle Bennett broke a BMX record by winning seven pro races in a row. He was a BMX world champion in both 2002 and 2003.

Bennett started racing BMX when he was 5 years old. Bennett was not an overnight success. He spent years as an amateur. At the 2001 Summer X Games, he came in 16th. But Bennett did not hang up his helmet. He kept racing. Now he is one of the new stars of downhill BMX racing.

ALICE JUNG

Alice Jung wanted to be a mountain bike racer. But she thought the bikes were too expensive. She bought a BMX bike instead. Buying a BMX bike was a good decision for Jung. Within six years, she was the number one female BMX rider.

Kyle Bennett is a BMX pro who also rides in downhill BMX races.

Alice Jung became the world's top female BMX rider.

CHRISTOPHE LEVEQUE

Christophe Leveque started racing BMX in 1987. He was 14 years old. A year later, he won his first major BMX race. Now in his 30s, Leveque is still a great rider.

Leveque has suffered injuries from BMX racing. In 2002, he hurt his back. He couldn't race for the whole season. He had surgery to fix his back and raced again in 2003. Leveque has won more than 100 races in his career.

Christophe Leveque has had a long BMX racing career.

Randy Stumpfhauser (left) takes a top line to pass during a race.

RANDY "STUMPY" STUMPFHAUSER

Randy Stumpfhauser started racing BMX when he was 9 years old. He turned pro at 18. Today, he's among the best racers in the world.

Stumpfhauser's BMX career wasn't always easy. He hurt both his knees and had to have surgery to repair the damage. Stumpfhauser worked hard to get back to the top of BMX racing. He came back to win a world championship race in 2002.

GLOSSARY

advertising (AD-ver-tize-ing)—when riders promote companies' products

amateur (AM-uh-tur)—an athlete who usually does not earn a living from competing in a sport

asphalt (ASS-fawlt)—a black, tarlike substance that is mixed with sand and gravel to make roads

berm (BURM)—a high banked turn on a BMX track

chromoly (kro-MOL-ee)—a mixture of metals used to make bike frames

gate (GATE)—a long metal frame that racers start on; gates drop down at the beginning of a race.

momentum (moh-MEN-tuhm)—the force or speed that a bike has when it is moving

nylon (NYE-lon)—a strong fiber used to make clothing; BMX leathers are made of nylon.

sponsor (SPON-sur)—a company that pays riders to advertise its products

traction (TRAK-shuhn)—the gripping power that BMX tires have against the ground

READ MORE

Blomquist, Christopher. *BMX in the X Games.* A Kid's Guide to the X Games. New York: PowerKids Press, 2003.

Firestone, Mary. *Extreme Downhill BMX Moves.* Behind the Moves. Mankato, Minn.: Capstone Press, 2004.

Wingate, Brian. *BMX Bicycle Racing: Techniques and Tricks.* Rad Sports. New York: Rosen, 2003.

INTERNET SITES

FactHound offers a safe, fun way to find Internet sites related to this book. All of the sites on FactHound have been researched by our staff.

Here's how:

1. Visit *www.facthound.com*
2. Type in this special code **0736827099** for age-appropriate sites. Or enter a search word related to this book for a more general search.
3. Click on the **Fetch It** button.

FactHound will fetch the best sites for you!

INDEX